delicious diabetic recipes

Quick & Easy Dinners

quick & easy dinners

Penne Pasta with Chunky Tomato Sauce and Spinach

8 ounces multigrain penne pasta
2 cups spicy marinara sauce
1 large ripe tomato, chopped (about 1½ cups)
4 cups packed baby spinach or torn spinach leaves
¼ cup grated Parmesan cheese
¼ cup chopped fresh basil

1. Cook pasta according to package directions, omitting salt.

2. Meanwhile, cook marinara sauce and tomato in medium saucepan over medium heat 3 to 4 minutes or until hot and bubbly, stirring occasionally. Turn off heat; stir in spinach.

3. Drain pasta; return to same saucepan. Add tomato mixture; toss to combine. Divide evenly among 8 serving bowls; top with cheese and basil.　　　　　　　　　*Makes 8 servings*

Nutrients per Serving: ¾ cup
Calories: 171, **Calories from Fat:** 14%, **Total Fat:** 3g,
Saturated Fat: 1g, **Cholesterol:** 4mg, **Sodium:** 319mg,
Carbohydrate: 29g, **Fiber:** 4g, **Protein:** 7g

Dietary Exchanges: 1 Vegetable, 1½ Starch, ½ Fat

Skillet Chicken Creole

1 small red onion, chopped
1 small red bell pepper, chopped
1 jalapeño pepper,* seeded and minced
2 cups no-salt-added crushed tomatoes
¼ teaspoon salt (optional)
⅛ teaspoon black pepper
12 ounces boneless skinless chicken breasts,
    cut into strips

*Jalapeño peppers can sting and irritate the skin, so wear rubber gloves when handling peppers and do not touch your eyes.

1. Spray large nonstick skillet with nonstick cooking spray; heat over medium heat. Add onion, bell pepper and jalapeño; cook and stir over medium heat 5 to 10 minutes or until vegetables are tender. Stir in tomatoes, salt, if desired, and black pepper.

2. Stir in chicken. Reduce heat to low; cover and simmer 12 to 15 minutes or until chicken is cooked through.

Makes 4 servings

Variation: If your diet plan permits, serve over brown rice. A ⅓-cup serving would add approximately 71 calories, less than 1g total fat, no satuated fat or cholesterol, 2g protein, 15g carbohydrate, 1g fiber and 3mg sodium.

Nutrients per Serving: 1 cup
Calories: 139, **Calories from Fat:** 7%, **Total Fat:** 1g,
Saturated Fat: <1g, **Cholesterol:** 49mg, **Sodium:** 96mg,
Carbohydrate: 11g, **Fiber:** 3g, **Protein:** 21g

Dietary Exchanges: 2 Vegetable, 2 Meat

Steak Diane with Cremini Mushrooms

2 beef tenderloin steaks (4 ounces each), cut ¾ inch thick
¼ teaspoon black pepper
⅓ cup sliced shallots or chopped onion
4 ounces cremini (brown or baby portobello) mushrooms, sliced *or* 1 (4-ounce) package sliced mixed wild mushrooms
1½ tablespoons Worcestershire sauce
1 tablespoon Dijon mustard

1. Lightly spray large nonstick skillet with nonstick cooking spray; heat over medium-high heat. Add steaks; sprinkle with pepper. Cook steaks 3 minutes per side for medium-rare or until desired doneness. Transfer steaks to plate; set aside.

2. Spray same skillet with cooking spray; place over medium heat. Add shallots; cook and stir 2 minutes. Add mushrooms; cook and stir 3 minutes. Add Worcestershire sauce and mustard; cook and stir 1 minute.

3. Return steaks and any accumulated juices to skillet; heat through, turning once. Transfer steaks to serving plates; top with mushroom mixture. *Makes 2 servings*

Nutrients per Serving: ½ of total recipe
Calories: 239, **Calories from Fat:** 35%, **Total Fat:** 9g,
Saturated Fat: 3g, **Cholesterol:** 70mg, **Sodium:** 302mg,
Carbohydrate: 10g, **Fiber:** 1g, **Protein:** 28g

Dietary Exchanges: 1 Vegetable, 4 Meat

Tuna Steaks with Pineapple and Tomato Salsa

1 medium tomato, chopped
1 can (8 ounces) pineapple chunks in juice, drained and chopped
2 tablespoons chopped fresh cilantro
1 tablespoon minced red onion
1 jalapeño pepper,* seeded and minced
½ teaspoon grated lime peel
2 teaspoons lime juice
4 tuna steaks (4 ounces each)
½ teaspoon salt
⅛ teaspoon black pepper
2 teaspoons olive oil

Jalapeño peppers can sting and irritate the skin, so wear rubber gloves when handling peppers and do not touch your eyes.

1. For salsa, combine tomato, pineapple, cilantro, onion, jalapeño, lime peel and lime juice in medium bowl.

2. Sprinkle tuna with salt and black pepper. Heat oil in large nonstick skillet over medium-high heat. Add tuna; cook 2 to 3 minutes per side for medium-rare or to desired degree of doneness. Serve with salsa. *Makes 4 servings*

Nutrients per Serving: 1 tuna steak and ½ cup salsa
Calories: 228, **Calories from Fat:** 32%, **Total Fat:** 8g,
Saturated Fat: 2g, **Cholesterol:** 43mg, **Sodium:** 338mg,
Carbohydrate: 11g, **Fiber:** 1g, **Protein:** 27g

Dietary Exchanges: 2 Vegetable, 3 Meat, 1½ Fat

Apple-Cherry Glazed Pork Chops

¼ to ½ **teaspoon dried thyme**
⅛ **teaspoon salt**
⅛ **teaspoon black pepper**
 2 **boneless pork loin chops (3 ounces each),**
    trimmed of fat
⅔ **cup unsweetened apple juice**
½ **small apple, sliced**
 2 **tablespoons sliced green onion**
 2 **tablespoons dried tart cherries**
 1 **tablespoon water**
 1 **teaspoon cornstarch**

1. Combine thyme, salt and pepper in small bowl; rub onto both sides of pork chops. Spray large skillet with olive oil cooking spray. Add pork chops; cook over medium heat 3 to 5 minutes or until barely pink in center, turning once. Remove chops from skillet; keep warm.

2. Add apple juice, apple slices, green onion and cherries to same skillet. Simmer, uncovered, 2 to 3 minutes or until apple and onion are tender.

3. Combine water and cornstarch in small bowl; stir into skillet. Bring to a boil; cook and stir until thickened. Spoon over pork chops.   *Makes 2 servings*

Nutrients per Serving: 1 pork chop with ½ cup apple-cherry mixture
Calories: 243, **Calories from Fat:** 31%, **Total Fat:** 8g,
Saturated Fat: 3g, **Cholesterol:** 40mg, **Sodium:** 191mg,
Carbohydrate: 23g, **Fiber:** 1g, **Protein:** 19g

Dietary Exchanges: 1½ Fruit, 2 Meat, 1½ Fat

Chicken and Spinach Salad

12 ounces chicken tenders
4 cups shredded stemmed spinach
2 cups washed and torn romaine lettuce
1 large grapefruit, peeled and sectioned
8 thin slices red onion, separated into rings
2 tablespoons crumbled blue cheese
½ cup frozen citrus blend concentrate, thawed
¼ cup prepared fat-free Italian salad dressing
Assorted fresh greens (optional)

1. Cut chicken into 2×½-inch strips. Spray large nonstick skillet with nonstick cooking spray; heat over medium heat. Add chicken; cook and stir 5 minutes or until chicken is cooked through. Remove from skillet; set aside.

2. Divide spinach, lettuce, grapefruit, onion, cheese and chicken among 4 salad plates. Combine citrus blend concentrate and Italian dressing in small bowl; drizzle over salads. *Makes 4 servings*

Nutrients per Serving: 2 cups salad
Calories: 218, **Calories from Fat:** 15%, **Total Fat:** 4g,
Saturated Fat: 1g, **Cholesterol:** 55mg, **Sodium:** 361mg,
Carbohydrate: 23g, **Fiber:** 3g, **Protein:** 23g

Dietary Exchanges: 2 Vegetable, 1 Fruit, 2½ Meat

Italian-Style Meat Loaf

    1 can (6 ounces) no-salt-added tomato paste
    ½ cup water
    ½ cup dry red wine
    1 teaspoon minced garlic
    ½ teaspoon dried basil
    ½ teaspoon dried oregano
    ¼ teaspoon salt
    12 ounces 95% lean ground beef
    12 ounces 93% lean ground turkey
    1 cup fresh whole wheat bread crumbs
        (2 slices whole wheat bread)
    ½ cup shredded zucchini
    ¼ cup cholesterol-free egg substitute *or* 2 egg whites

1. Preheat oven to 350°F. Combine tomato paste, water, wine, garlic, basil, oregano and salt in small saucepan; bring to a boil. Reduce heat to low; simmer, uncovered, 15 minutes.

2. Combine beef, turkey, bread crumbs, zucchini, egg substitute and ½ cup tomato mixture in large bowl; mix lightly. Shape into loaf; place in ungreased 9×5-inch loaf pan.

3. Bake 45 minutes. Drain fat. Spread ½ cup tomato mixture over top of loaf. Bake 15 minutes more or until cooked through (160°F in center). Transfer to serving platter. Cool 10 minutes. Cut into 8 slices. *Makes 8 servings*

Nutrients per Serving: 1 slice (⅛ of total recipe)
Calories: 187, **Calories from Fat:** 11%, **Total Fat:** 6g,
Saturated Fat: 2g, **Cholesterol:** 56mg, **Sodium:** 212mg,
Carbohydrate: 12g, **Fiber:** 2g, **Protein:** 19g

Dietary Exchanges: 1 Starch, 2 Meat

Roast Turkey Breast with Apple-Corn Bread Stuffing

        1 medium onion, chopped
    1¼ cups fat-free reduced-sodium chicken broth
        1 package (8 ounces) corn bread stuffing mix
        1 Granny Smith apple, diced
    ¾ teaspoon dried sage, divided
    ¾ teaspoon dried thyme, divided
        1 boneless turkey breast (1½ pounds)
        1 teaspoon paprika
    ¼ teaspoon black pepper

1. Preheat oven to 450°F. Coat 1½-quart casserole with nonstick cooking spray; set aside. Coat large saucepan with cooking spray; heat over medium heat. Add onion; cook and stir 5 minutes. Add broth; bring to a simmer. Stir in stuffing mix, apple, ¼ teaspoon sage and ¼ teaspoon thyme. Transfer mixture to prepared casserole; set aside.

2. Coat shallow roasting pan with cooking spray. Place turkey breast in pan, skin side up; coat with cooking spray. Mix paprika, remaining ½ teaspoon sage, ½ teaspoon thyme and pepper in small bowl; sprinkle over turkey. Spray lightly with cooking spray.

3. Roast turkey 15 minutes. *Reduce oven temperature to 350°F.* Place stuffing in oven with turkey; roast 35 minutes or until internal temperature of turkey reaches 170°F when tested with meat thermometer inserted into thickest part of breast. Transfer turkey to cutting board; cover with foil and let stand 10 to 15 minutes before carving. (Internal temperature will rise 5° to 10°F during stand time.) Remove stuffing from oven; cover to keep warm. Carve turkey into thin slices; serve with stuffing.

Makes 7 servings

Nutrients per Serving: ⅐ of total recipe
Calories: 260, **Calories from Fat:** 10%, **Total Fat:** 3g,
Saturated Fat: <1g, **Cholesterol:** 64mg, **Sodium:** 497mg,
Carbohydrate: 29g, **Fiber:** 6g, **Protein:** 28g

Dietary Exchanges: 2 Starch, 4 Meat

Crisp Lemony Baked Fish

1¼ cups crushed cornflakes
¼ cup shredded Parmesan cheese
2 tablespoons minced green onion
⅛ teaspoon black pepper
1 lemon
¼ cup cholesterol-free egg substitute
4 small haddock fillets (about 3 ounces each)

1. Preheat oven to 400°F. Line baking sheet with parchment paper.

2. Combine cornflakes, cheese, green onion and pepper in small bowl. Grate lemon peel; stir into cornflake mixture. Reserve lemon for serving. Spread cornflake mixture on plate. Pour egg substitute into shallow bowl.

3. Dip fish fillets into egg substitute, then into cornflake mixture; coat well on both sides. Place coated fillets on prepared baking sheet.

4. Bake about 10 minutes or until fish begins to flake when tested with fork. Cut reserved lemon into wedges; serve with fish. *Makes 4 servings*

Nutrients per Serving: 1 fish fillet
Calories: 209, **Calories from Fat:** 9%, **Total Fat:** 2g,
Saturated Fat: <1g, **Cholesterol:** 53mg, **Sodium:** 364mg,
Carbohydrate: 26g, **Fiber:** 1g, **Protein:** 22g

Dietary Exchanges: 2 Starch, 2 Meat

Chicken Skillet with Pearl Onions

½ **teaspoon salt**
½ **teaspoon onion powder**
½ **teaspoon garlic powder**
½ **teaspoon chili powder**
½ **teaspoon dried oregano**
4 **boneless skinless chicken breasts**
2 **cups water**
1 **pound small new potatoes**
8 **ounces fresh pearl onions, blanched and peeled, or**
   frozen pearl onions, thawed
2 **tablespoons olive oil**

1. Combine salt, onion powder, garlic powder, chili powder and oregano in small bowl. Sprinkle evenly over both sides of chicken. Cover and refrigerate.

2. Combine water, potatoes and onions in large nonstick skillet. Bring to a boil over medium-high heat. Cover and boil 12 minutes or until potatoes are tender when pierced with fork. Drain well; set aside.

3. Return skillet to medium-high heat; add 1 tablespoon oil. Add chicken. Cook 4 minutes; turn. Add potatoes and onions; drizzle with remaining 1 tablespoon oil. Cover; cook 4 to 5 minutes or until chicken is no longer pink in center and onions are slightly browned, stirring occasionally. Let stand 3 minutes before serving.   *Makes 4 servings*

Tip: Always use a spatula or tongs to turn chicken over during cooking. This prevents the surface from being pierced, keeping the natural juices sealed inside.

Nutrients per Serving: 1 chicken breast with 1 cup potatoes and onions
Calories: 302, **Calories from Fat:** 25%, **Total Fat:** 8g,
Saturated Fat: 1g, **Cholesterol:** 66mg, **Sodium:** 394mg,
Carbohydrate: 27g, **Fiber:** 3g, **Protein:** 29g

Dietary Exchanges: 2 Starch, 3 Meat, 1½ Fat

Asian Pork Tenderloin

½ cup garlic ginger marinade
¼ cup sliced green onions
1 pork tenderloin (about 1 pound)
1 tablespoon olive oil
1 red onion, cut into chunks
1 red bell pepper, cut into 1-inch pieces
1 zucchini, sliced ¼ inch thick

1. Place marinade and green onions in large resealable food storage bag. Add pork. Seal bag; turn to coat. Marinate in refrigerator 30 minutes or overnight.

2. Preheat oven to 425°F. Combine oil, red onion, bell pepper and zucchini in large bowl; toss to coat. Spread in roasting pan. Remove pork from bag and place on top of vegetables. Discard marinade.

3. Bake 20 to 25 minutes or until pork is barely pink in center (160°F). Remove pork to cutting board; loosely cover with foil and let stand 10 minutes before slicing. Serve pork with vegetables.

Makes 4 servings

Nutrients per Serving: ¼ of total recipe
Calories: 220, **Calories from Fat:** 20%, **Total Fat:** 5g,
Saturated Fat: 2g, **Cholesterol:** 75mg, **Sodium:** 540mg,
Carbohydrate: 15g, **Fiber:** 1g, **Protein:** 5g

Dietary Exchanges: 1 Vegetable, 3 Meat, 1 Fat

Mexican Casserole with Tortilla Chips

12 ounces lean ground turkey
1 bag (8 ounces) frozen bell pepper stir-fry mixture, thawed
1 can (about 14 ounces) no-salt-added stewed tomatoes
¾ teaspoon ground cumin
½ teaspoon salt (optional)
⅓ cup finely shredded reduced-fat sharp Cheddar cheese
2 ounces reduced-fat tortilla chips, lightly crushed

1. Spray large nonstick skillet with nonstick cooking spray. Cook turkey over medium heat until cooked through, stirring to break up meat. Add pepper mixture, tomatoes and cumin. Bring to a boil. Reduce heat; cover and simmer 20 minutes or until vegetables are tender.

2. Stir in salt, if desired. Sprinkle evenly with cheese and chips.

Makes 4 servings

Variation: Sprinkle chips into a casserole. Spread cooked turkey mixture evenly over the chips and top with cheese.

Nutrients per Serving: ¼ of total recipe
Calories: 244, **Calories from Fat:** 32%, **Total Fat:** 9g, **Saturated Fat:** 3g, **Cholesterol:** 60mg, **Sodium:** 236mg, **Carbohydrate:** 21g, **Fiber:** 3g, **Protein:** 23g

Dietary Exchanges: 1 Vegetable, 1 Starch, 2 Meat, 1 Fat

Oven-Fried Chicken

**4 boneless skinless chicken breasts
(about 4 ounces each)**
**4 small skinless chicken drumsticks
(about 2½ ounces each)**
3 tablespoons all-purpose flour
½ teaspoon poultry seasoning
¼ teaspoon garlic salt
¼ teaspoon black pepper
1½ cups cornflakes, crushed
1 tablespoon dried parsley flakes
1 egg white
1 tablespoon water

1. Preheat oven to 375°F. Trim fat from chicken. Spray large baking sheet with nonstick cooking spray.

2. Combine flour, poultry seasoning, garlic salt and pepper in resealable food storage bag. Combine cornflakes and parsley in small shallow bowl. Whisk egg white and water in small bowl.

3. Add chicken to flour mixture, 1 or 2 pieces at a time. Seal bag; shake until chicken is well coated. Remove chicken from bag, shaking off excess flour mixture. Dip into egg white mixture, coating all sides. Roll in crumb mixture. Place on prepared baking sheet. Repeat with remaining chicken, flour mixture, egg white mixture and crumb mixture. Lightly spray chicken pieces with nonstick cooking spray.

4. Bake breast pieces 18 to 20 minutes or until no longer pink in center. Bake drumsticks about 25 minutes or until cooked through and juices run clear. *Makes 4 servings*

Nutrients per Serving: 1 chicken breast and 1 drumstick
Calories: 314, **Calories from Fat:** 17%, **Total Fat:** 6g,
Saturated Fat: 2g, **Cholesterol:** 170mg, **Sodium:** 278mg,
Carbohydrate: 13g, **Fiber:** 1g, **Protein:** 50g

Dietary Exchanges: 1 Starch, 5 Meat

Gingered Shrimp and Vegetable Fried Skillet

8 ounces frozen medium or large shrimp, thawed, peeled and deveined
2 teaspoons minced fresh ginger
3 cloves garlic, minced
2 cups fresh sugar snap peas
1 red or yellow bell pepper, cut into thin 1-inch strips
3 tablespoons reduced-sodium soy sauce
1 package (8½ ounces) cooked brown rice
1 tablespoon dark sesame oil
¼ cup chopped fresh cilantro or green onions

1. Spray large nonstick skillet with nonstick cooking spray; heat over medium-high heat. Add shrimp, ginger and garlic; stir-fry 1 minute.

2. Add peas and bell pepper; stir-fry 4 minutes or until shrimp are pink and opaque and vegetables are crisp-tender. Stir in soy sauce; stir-fry 1 minute.

3. Add rice; stir-fry 2 minutes or until heated through. Turn off heat; stir in sesame oil and cilantro.   *Makes 4 servings*

Nutrients per Serving: 1¼ cups
Calories: 201, **Calories from Fat:** 22%, **Total Fat:** 5g,
Saturated Fat: 1g, **Cholesterol:** 86mg, **Sodium:** 540mg,
Carbohydrate: 22g, **Fiber:** 3g, **Protein:** 16g

Dietary Exchanges: 1 Vegetable, 1 Starch, 2 Meat, 1 Fat